John Baptist de la Salle

Caring Teacher and Mentor

1651–1719
Born in Reims, France
Feast Day: April 7
Community Role: Teacher

Text by Barbara Yoffie
Illustrated by Jeff Albrecht

Liguori
ONE LIGUORI DRIVE
LIGUORI MO 63057-9999

Dedication

To my family:
my parents Jim and Peg,
my husband Bill,
our son Sam and daughter-in-law Erin,
and our precious grandchildren
Ben, Lucas, and Andrew

To all the children I have had the privilege of
teaching throughout the years.

Imprimi Potest:
Stephen T. Rehrauer, CSsR, Provincial
Denver Province, the Redemptorists

Published by Liguori Publications
Liguori, Missouri 63057

To order, visit Liguori.org or call 800-325-9521.

p ISBN 978-0-7648-2553-8
e ISBN 978-0-7648-7004-0

Liguori Publications, a nonprofit corporation, is an apostolate of the
Redemptorists. To learn more about the Redemptorists, visit Redemptorists.com.

Printed in the United States of America
19 18 17 16 15 / 5 4 3 2 1
First Edition

Dear Parents and Teachers:

Saints and Me! is a series of children's books about saints, with six books in each set. The first set, *Saints of North America,* honors holy men and women who blessed and served the land we call home. The second set, *Saints of Christmas,* includes heavenly heroes who inspire us through Advent and Christmas and teach us to love the Infant Jesus. The third set, *Saints for Families,* introduces saints who modeled God's love within and for the domestic Church.

Saints for Communities explores six individuals from different times and places who served Jesus through their various roles and professions. Saint John Baptist de la Salle taught children and founded a familiar educational system. Saint Joan of Arc helped to bring peace to the country of France. The Apostle Matthew was a tax collector before deciding to follow Jesus. The Apostle Thomas preached and built churches. Saint Cecilia sang hymns to Jesus in her heart. And Michael the Archangel is well-known for his protection.

Which saint doubted Jesus' resurrection? Which one fought a heavenly battle? Which saint heard heavenly voices? Who sold everything he owned? Which saint was first named Levi? Which saint was married against her will? Find out in the *Saints for Communities* set—part of the *Saints and Me!* series—and help your child connect to the lives of the saints.

Introduce your children or students to the *Saints and Me!* series as they:

—**READ** about the lives of the saints and are inspired by their stories.

—**PRAY** to the saints for their intercession.

—**CELEBRATE** the saints and relate them to their lives.

saints of communities

 John Baptist
Teacher

 Joan of Arc
Soldier

 Matthew
Banker

 Thomas
Construction worker

 Cecilia
Musician

 Michael
Police officer

John Baptist de la Salle was born in France more than 300 years ago. He was the oldest son in the de la Salle family. His parents taught him to love God. As John grew, so did his faith.

In those days, there were many poor people living in the country and in city slums. There were wars, and people were sick. Many families did not have enough food to eat. Poor children could not go to school.

John was very lucky. His family was not poor. They had plenty of food and lived in a big house. They had everything they needed. John was a happy child with lots of friends.

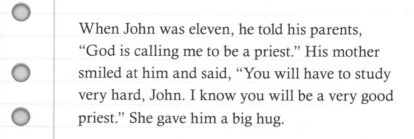

When John was eleven, he told his parents, "God is calling me to be a priest." His mother smiled at him and said, "You will have to study very hard, John. I know you will be a very good priest." She gave him a big hug.

John went to Paris, France, to study at the seminary there. He prayed, studied, and grew closer to God. But the next year, his mother died, and his father died the year after that! John went home to take care of his brothers and sisters and run the household. With a lot of work and help from others, he became a priest and served the cathedral in the city of Reims.

Father John celebrated Mass and worked with poor children. He enjoyed helping others in need. People liked Father John because he was kind and good.

Every morning, Father John prayed for the children in the neighborhood. "Dear God, the children are so poor. They have no money and cannot go to school. How can I help them?" God soon answered his prayers.

One day a man asked Father John, "Would you like to help me start a school for poor children in my town?" Father John thought for a while. It was not the work he thought he would do or wanted to do. *"But this must be God's plan for me,"* thought Father John. So he said "yes," and he did not start one school—he started two!

There was a lot of work to do. Father John sold everything he had and gave the money to the poor. He began to spend all his time working with the teachers in a special training college. He talked to them and taught them how to plan lessons. He wrote books. "Care for all your students. Show them respect and love. Teaching is God's work," he said. "We must try very hard."

Later, Father John started a community of religious brothers to teach poor children. It was called the Brothers of the Christian Schools, or Christian Brothers. The brothers wore black robes with a white collar. They read from the Bible and prayed every day. They taught children how to live good, Christian lives. Best of all, the schools were free!

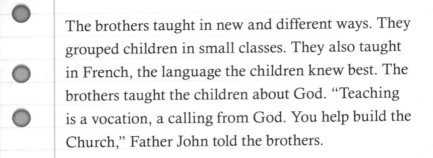

The brothers taught in new and different ways. They grouped children in small classes. They also taught in French, the language the children knew best. The brothers taught the children about God. "Teaching is a vocation, a calling from God. You help build the Church," Father John told the brothers.

Some people did not like what Father John was doing. They did not like free schools or the way he taught. But Father John kept working. He wanted very good schools for all the children.

Father John's faith was strong. He prayed and trusted God. God was always with him, guiding him to do the right thing.

After Father John died, the Brothers of the Christian Schools continued the work he began. They started other schools throughout France. Today the Christian Brothers work all over the world as teachers, social workers, and counselors. They give retreats and live in the spirit of their founder. God guides their good and holy work.

John Baptist

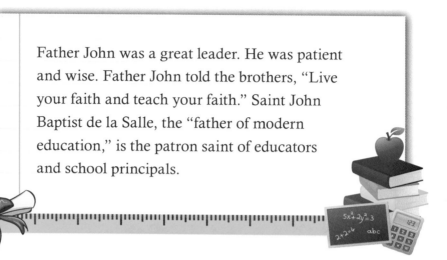

Father John was a great leader. He was patient and wise. Father John told the brothers, "Live your faith and teach your faith." Saint John Baptist de la Salle, the "father of modern education," is the patron saint of educators and school principals.

God is with you every day.
He will guide you on your way.

Dear God.

I love you very much.

Saint John Baptist de

la Salle loved you, too.

He helped teachers

and poor children.

Help me to open

my heart to those

in need.

Amen.

NEW WORDS (Glossary)

Brothers: Men who take religious vows and live in community but are not priests

Cathedral: The highest, leading church of a city or area, where the bishop or archbishop presides

Founder: The person or group who creates and starts an organization, community, or movement

The Institute of the Brothers of the Christian Schools: A community of consecrated laymen (religious brothers) founded in 1680 by Saint John Baptist de la Salle.

Mentor: Someone who gives advice and encouragement to a less-experienced, often younger, person; a trusted counselor

Seminary: A school where men train to be priests

Slums: An area where poor people live

Vocation: A call from God to serve him in a special way

The Institute of the Brothers of Christian Schools goes by many names: De La Salle Christian Brothers, Lasallian Brothers, Lasallian Institute, and Christian Brothers. It is *not* the same as the Congregation of Christian Brothers founded by Edmund Rice and sometimes called Irish Christian Brothers.

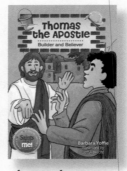